NATIONAL GEOGRAPHIC

T0069695

I Help in the Garden

Jim Westie

The wheelbarrow is **heavy**.

Now the wheelbarrow is **light**.

The pot is **heavy**.

Now the pot is **light**.

The watering can is **heavy**.

Now the watering can is **light**.

Now the basket is **heavy**.